You Go Girl

YOU GO GIRL

An Hachette UK Company
www.hachette.co.uk

Summersdale Publishers
Part of Octopus Publishing Group Limited
Carmelite House
50 Victoria Embankment
LONDON
EC4Y 0DZ
UK

www.summersdale.com

This FSC® label means that materials and other controlled sources used for the product have been responsibly sourced

The authorized representative in the EEA is Hachette Ireland, 8 Castlecourt Centre, Dublin 15, D15 XTP3, Ireland (email: info@hbgi.ie)

Printed and bound in China

ISBN: 978-1-83799-767-1
eISBN: 978-1-83799-768-8

To...

From...

You are your best thing.

Toni Morrison

You don't have
to wait to be
confident. Just do
it and eventually
the confidence
will follow.

Carrie Fisher

You can
have it all

It's very important for women to lift each other up.

Kamala Harris

YOU ARE NEVER TOO SMALL TO MAKE A DIFFERENCE.

Greta Thunberg

I am no bird, and no net ensnares me; I am a free human being with an independent will.

Charlotte Brontë

Let determination replace your doubt

There's nothing like a powerful woman walking into a room; her presence is like nothing else.

Venus Williams

I raise up my voice
- not so that I can
shout, but so that
those without a
voice can be heard.

Malala Yousafzai

YOUR POTENTIAL IS LIMITLESS

Other women who are killing it should motivate you, thrill you, challenge you and inspire you.

Taylor Swift

Every great dream begins with a dreamer.

Power is not
given to you.
You have to
take it.

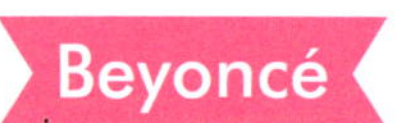

Maybe it's easier than you think

Always be a first-rate version of yourself instead of a second-rate version of somebody else.

Judy Garland

When you take
care of yourself,
you're a better
person for others.

Solange Knowles

CELEBRATE YOURSELF

Embrace what makes you unique, even if it makes others uncomfortable.

Janelle Monáe

I AM A WOMAN AND I GET TO DEFINE WHAT THAT MEANS.

Swati Sharma

The most common way people give up their power is by thinking they don't have any.

Alice Walker

FIGURE OUT WHAT HAPPINESS FEELS LIKE TO YOU

Take the wisdoms
of the women
in this world
and keep them
at your side.

Beanie Feldstein

It takes a great
deal of courage
and independence
to decide to
design your own
image instead
of the one that
society rewards.

Germaine Greer

Draw
your own
boundaries

Women are strong and fragile. Women are beautiful and ugly. We are soft-spoken and loud, all at once.

Lady Gaga

Women are intrinsically powerful.

Barbra Streisand

My mother did
not raise me to
ask permission
to lead.

Keep your
heart set on
your dreams

It's about owning your power, embracing your womanhood.

Alicia Keys

I don't think of myself as anything except me.

Billie Eilish

DO IT FOR YOURSELF

I refuse to believe that you cannot be both compassionate and strong.

Jacinda Ardern

THE ONE PERSON WHO WILL NEVER LEAVE US, WHOM WE WILL NEVER LOSE, IS OURSELF.

bell hooks

Think like a queen. A queen is not afraid to fail.

Oprah Winfrey

Have
no fear

Feminism isn't about making women stronger; women are already strong. It's about changing the way the world perceives that strength.

G. D. Anderson

I must undertake
to love myself
and respect myself
as though my very
life depends
upon self-love
and self-respect.

June Jordan

LEARN, EVOLVE, BLOSSOM

I'll tell you what freedom is to me: no fear!

Nina Simone

There is no gate,
no lock, no bolt
that you can set
upon the freedom
of my mind.

Virginia Woolf

You can start late, look different, be uncertain and still succeed.

GO AFTER THE VISION, NOT VALIDATION

If you prioritize yourself, you are going to save yourself.

Gabrielle Union

If they don't give
you a seat at the
table, bring a
folding chair.

Shirley Chisholm

You are
powerful

When women affirm women, it unlocks our power. It gives us permission to shine brighter.

Elaine Welteroth

I SEE ALL WOMEN AS SMART, GIFTED AND TOUGH.

Zaha Hadid

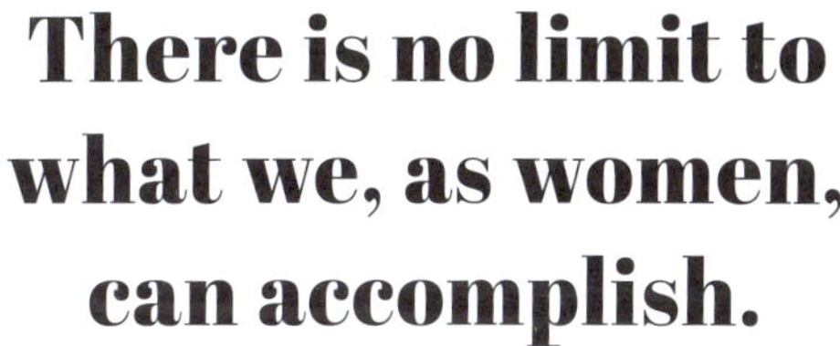

There is no limit to
what we, as women,
can accomplish.

Michelle Obama

Well-being begins within

It takes a certain
grace, strength,
intelligence,
fearlessness
and the nerve
to never take no
for an answer.

Rihanna

They'll tell you
you're too loud,
that you need
to wait your
turn and ask
the right people
for permission.
Do it anyway.

Alexandria Ocasio-Cortez

YOU CAN DO
ANYTHING
YOU
SET YOUR
MIND TO

My courage always rises at every attempt to intimidate me.

Jane Austen

You have
to believe
in yourself
when no one
else does.

Serena Williams

There is no
greater pillar
of stability than
a strong, free
and educated
woman.

Stand up for what you believe in

Power has to come from inside. It has to come from knowing who you are.

Jane Fonda

Let go of
who you think
you're supposed
to be; embrace
who you are.

Brené Brown

BE PROUD OF ALL YOU HAVE ACHIEVED AND ALL YOU WILL ACHIEVE

If you don't see
a clear path for
what you want,
sometimes you
have to make
it yourself.

Mindy Kaling

FILL YOUR LIFE WITH WOMEN THAT EMPOWER YOU, THAT HELP YOU BELIEVE IN YOUR MAGIC.

Nikita Gill

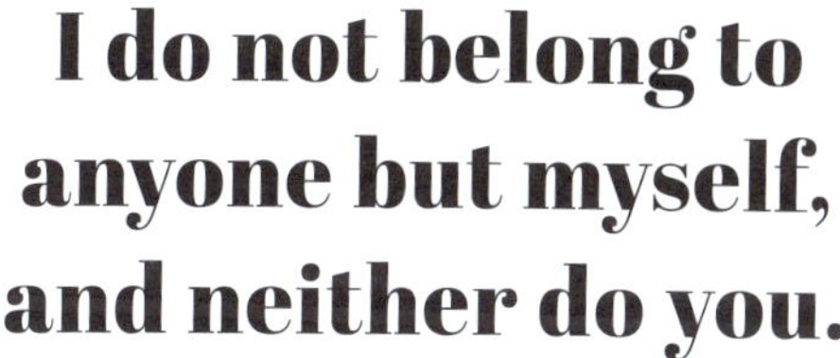

I do not belong to anyone but myself, and neither do you.

Ariana Grande

MAKE YOURSELF A PRIORITY

A strong woman is something to be celebrated and not feared.

Jameela Jamil

Above anything
else, stay true
to yourself.

Gillian Anderson

You are already whole

I'm not afraid of storms, for I'm learning how to sail my ship.

Louisa May Alcott

I'm tough, I'm ambitious and I know exactly what I want.

Madonna

Girls should
never be afraid
to be smart.

Emma Watson

Embrace yourself as you are

Always be in your strength, always use your voice, and don't let anyone make you quiet.

Amandla Stenberg

I love myself
when I am laughing...
and then again when
I am looking mean
and impressive.

Zora Neale Hurston

YOU CAN
DO GREAT
THINGS

The most important relationship is with yourself.

Bella Hadid

IT TAKES BOLD VOICES AND BOLD STEPS TO MAKE THINGS CHANGE.

Megan Rapinoe

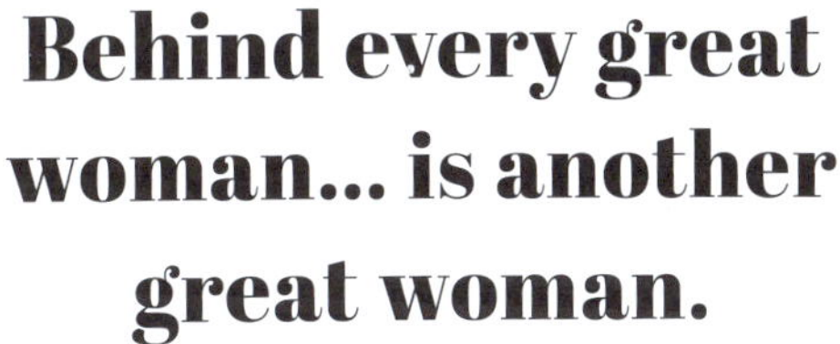

Behind every great woman... is another great woman.

Kate Hodges

Happiness is a journey, not a destination

Keep dreaming.
Keep pushing.

Little Simz

I love to see a
young girl go out
and grab the world
by the lapels.

Maya Angelou

NEVER FORGET TO MAKE YOUR VOICE HEARD

A woman
with a voice is,
by definition,
a strong woman.

Melinda French Gates

We must have perseverance and above all confidence in ourselves.

Marie Curie

The beauty of
being a feminist
is that you get
to be whatever
you want.

GO FOR IT, GIRL

Don't settle for average. Bring your best to the moment.

Angela Bassett

The most important
thing one woman
can do for another
is to illuminate
and expand her
sense of actual
possibilities.

Adrienne Rich

You've got this

**Do not
live someone
else's life and
someone else's
idea of what
womanhood is.
Womanhood
is you.**

Viola Davis

FIND OUT WHO YOU ARE AND DO IT ON PURPOSE.

Dolly Parton

When women speak truly they speak subversively.

Ursula K. Le Guin

Embrace your powerful girl era

I am learning
every day to allow
the space between
where I am and
where I want to be
to inspire me and
not terrify me.

Tracee Ellis Ross

You draw your own box. You introduce yourself as who you are… You create the identity you want for yourself.

Meghan, Duchess of Sussex

BELIEVE IN
YOURSELF
AND
ANYTHING
CAN HAPPEN

You have to act as if it were possible to radically transform the world. And you have to do it all the time.

Angela Davis

I have not ever
been interested
in being invisible,
in being erased.

Laverne Cox

One can never consent to creep when one feels an impulse to soar.

Helen Keller

Be bold, unapologetic and authentic

A wise woman wishes to be no one's enemy; a wise woman refuses to be anyone's victim.

Maya Angelou

It took me quite
a long time to
develop a voice,
and now that I have
it, I am not going
to be silent.

Madeleine Albright

YOU
DESERVE
TO BE
LISTENED
TO

Deal with yourself as an individual worthy of respect and make everyone else deal with you the same way.

Nikki Giovanni

STRONG WOMEN: MAY WE KNOW THEM, MAY WE RAISE THEM, MAY WE BE THEM.

P!nk

I don't get my
inspiration from
books or a painting.
I get it from the
women I meet.

Carolina Herrera

YOUR TRUE SELF IS YOUR MOST BEAUTIFUL SELF

Well-behaved women seldom make history.

Laurel Thatcher Ulrich

When I dare to
be powerful, to
use my strength
in the service
of my vision,
then it becomes
less and less
important whether
I am afraid.

Audre Lorde

Know
your worth

What you have inside is much more beautiful than what's on the outside.

Selena Gomez

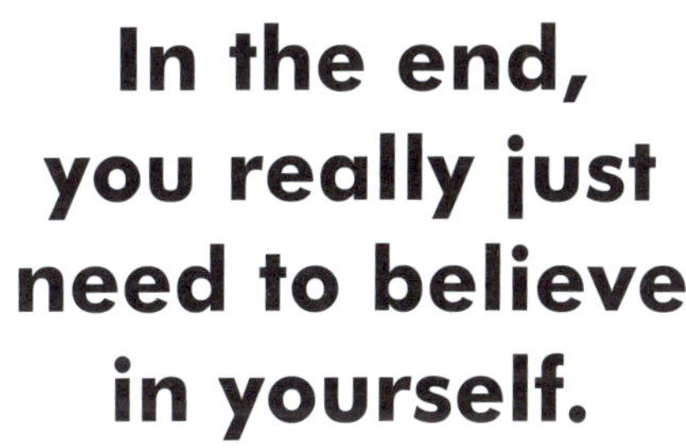
In the end,
you really just
need to believe
in yourself.

Diana Ross

We are
always
stronger
together.

Practise
limitless
self-love

If I wait for someone else to validate my existence, it will mean that I'm short-changing myself.

Zanele Muholi

Never let anyone
tell you you can't
do something
when you can.

Gabby Douglas

TRUST YOURSELF

Woman must not accept; she must challenge.

Margaret Sanger

WHAT PEOPLE SAY ISN'T GOING TO STOP ME. I HAVE TO DO THINGS FOR MYSELF.

Kate Moss

I've just never cared what people think. It's more if I'm happy and I'm confident and feeling good.

Kelly Clarkson

Imperfections mean individuality

**You can be
the lead in
your own life.**

Kerry Washington

Believe in
yourself and be
proud of who you
are. Don't let
anyone tell you
differently.

June Sarpong

THE ONLY VALIDATION THAT MATTERS IS YOUR OWN

Dreaming is free. And it's fun, so do it.

Lupita Nyong'o

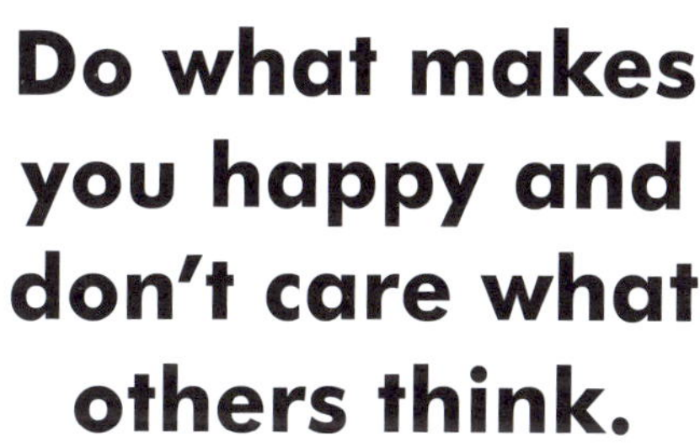

Do what makes you happy and don't care what others think.

Demi Lovato

You are
limitless.
We are *all*
limitless!

Jennifer Lopez

KEEP ON BEING AMAZING

Every woman has the right to become herself and do whatever she needs to do.

Ani DiFranco

You are
powerful and
your voice
matters.

Kamala Harris

Be your own heroine

Find a sense of self because, with that, you can do anything.

Angelina Jolie

I THRIVE ON OBSTACLES. IF I'M TOLD THAT IT CAN'T BE TOLD, THEN I PUSH HARDER.

Issa Rae

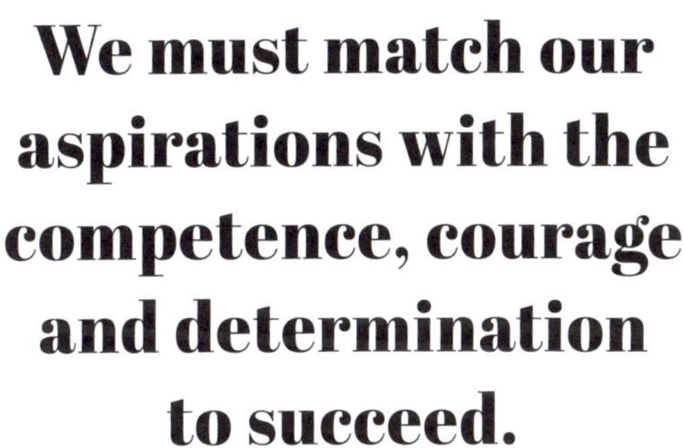

We must match our aspirations with the competence, courage and determination to succeed.

Rosalyn Sussman Yalow

Never forget
to listen to
your heart

My mission, should I choose to accept it, is to find peace with exactly who and what I am.

Anaïs Nin

We're so much more
powerful together
as well when we
look out for each
other, when we
uplift each other,
when we protect
each other.

Zendaya

KEEP DOING YOU!

Be bold. Be brave enough to be your true self.

Queen Latifah

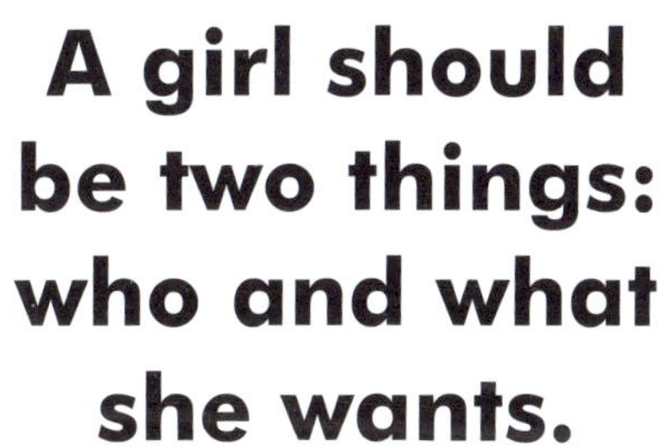

Coco Chanel

Never settle
for less, know
your worth
and be bold!

You are already enough

Once you really
know yourself,
can't nobody
tell you nothing
about you.

Megan Thee Stallion

I got here because
I had guts and I
was never afraid
to be the first.

Halima Aden

BE A DREAMER AND A GO-GETTER

May we give to each other and to the world what we would like to see more of.

Gisele Bündchen

I DON'T GO BY THE RULE BOOK...

I LEAD FROM THE HEART, NOT THE HEAD.

Diana, Princess of Wales

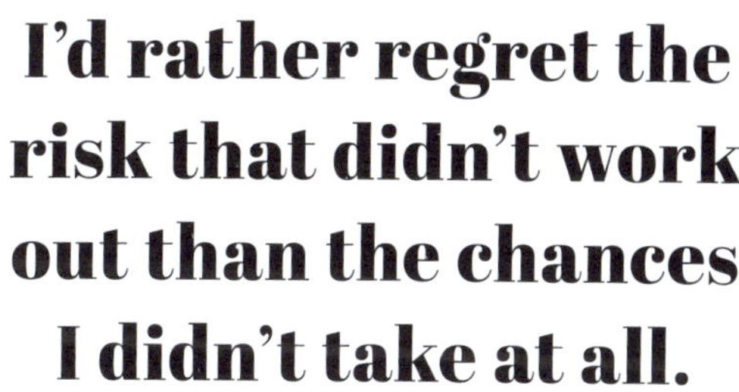

I'd rather regret the risk that didn't work out than the chances I didn't take at all.

Simone Biles

YOU ARE AN UNSTOPPABLE FORCE

**Be courageous.
Challenge
orthodoxy.
Stand up for
what you
believe in.**

Amal Clooney

Whoever you are,
however you are,
you are equally
valid, equally
justified and
equally beautiful.

Juno Dawson

You are
stronger
than you
realize

Every woman's success should be an inspiration to another. We're strongest when we cheer each other on.

Serena Williams

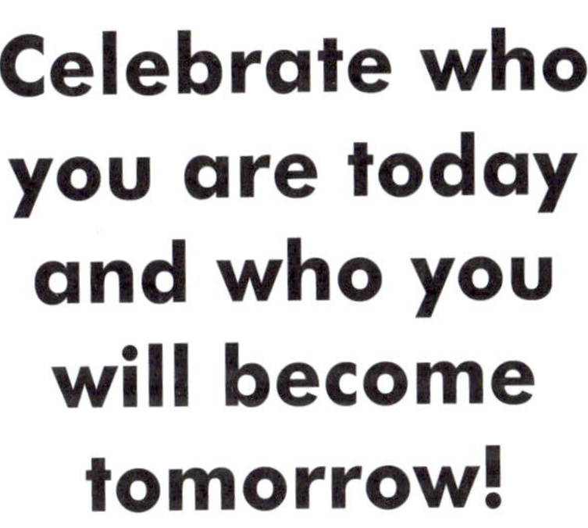

Celebrate who you are today and who you will become tomorrow!

Kris Jenner

Where there
is a woman,
there is magic.

YOU GO GIRL

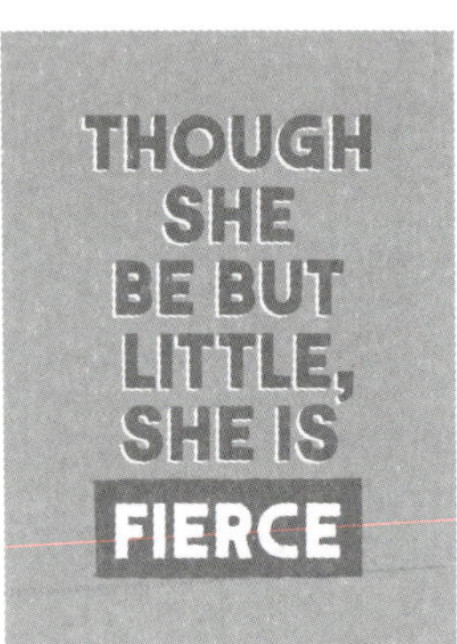

THOUGH SHE BE BUT LITTLE, SHE IS FIERCE

Powerful Quotes for Powerful Women

ISBN: 978-1-83799-765-7 • Hardback

Unleash your whole potential with this punchy little book of feminist quotes and affirmations. Featuring words from a host of inspiring women, this compilation will remind you that you are forever fearless, fierce and fabulous!

BESTIE

The Perfect Gift to Celebrate Your BFF

ISBN: 978-1-83799-901-9 • Hardback

Your best friend is your whole world: the bubbles in your champagne, the one who lifts you up when you're feeling down and who fills your life with joy and sparkles. Celebrate your BFF with this fabulous collection of uplifting quotes and affirmations about the joys of being besties.

Have you enjoyed this book?
If so, find us on Facebook at
Summersdale Publishers, on
Twitter/X at **@Summersdale** and
on Instagram, TikTok and Bluesky at
@summersdalebooks and get in
touch. We'd love to hear from you!

www.summersdale.com